Fringe

poems by

Jennifer Burd

Finishing Line Press
Georgetown, Kentucky

Fringe

for All

ACKNOWLEDGMENTS

Grateful acknowledgment is given to the following publishers, and to the
publications in which the following poems have previously appeared:

"At Alan's Tent," "Encounter," "Sunday Dinner," "Luna/Because," and "Long,
Lonesome Lonely Road" were first published in *Daily Bread: A Portrait of Homeless
Men & Women of Lenawee County, Michigan*. Huron, Ohio: Bottom Dog Press, 2009.

"Encounter," "Sunday Dinner," and "Luna/Because," were published in their current
form in *Body and Echo*. Austin, Texas: Plain View Press, 2010.

"What the Body Says When There Is No Shelter," and "Your Dream Sleep" first
appeared in *Day's Late Blue*. Cincinnati, Ohio: Cherry Grove Collections, 2017.

"Prison Literature Class" first appeared in the anthology *A Constellation of Kisses*.
Diane Lockward, ed. West Caldwell, New Jersey: Terrapin Books, 2019.

"prison math class" [haiku], was first published in *Acorn: A Contemporary Journal of
Haiku*. Susan Antolin, ed. No. 44, Spring 2020.

Publisher: Leah Huete de Maines
Editor: Christen Kincaid
Cover Art: Jennifer Burd
Author Photo: Linda Navarro
Cover Design: Elizabeth Maines McCleavy

Order online: www.finishinglinepress.com
also available on amazon.com

Author inquiries and mail orders:
Finishing Line Press
PO Box 1626
Georgetown, Kentucky 40324
USA

Table of Contents

A Note to the Reader

By way of mirroring the layers of modern society and the fragmented experiences of those living on its fringes, this collection of poems is woven through with bits of dictionary definition, haiku, and quotes and statistics about homelessness and incarceration. The latter include publication dates for some of the statistics. Even as these dates recede into the distance, the trend is that the grim numbers continue to increase—but the issues and challenges, sadly, remain the same, whatever the numbers.

—Jennifer Burd, April 2022

1: Streets

Fringe

noun

1
a decorative border of thread, cord, or the like,
usually hanging from a raveled edge

the streets you walk all day resembling, or perhaps suggesting,
      your life diagrammed out to a dangling
                        participle

2
anything resembling or suggesting this

"You probably see them all over. Bands of tents set down in
a wooded area, flashes of blue tarp dangling from a freeway
overpass, or clusters of cardboard wrestled into shapes that will
provide some kind of shelter. They're small, ad hoc camps of
homeless people, and their numbers are growing."
        —Ari Cetron, *Seattle Magazine*, April 2015

Encounter

Sitting at the soup kitchen
lunch counter, I sip
coffee while Kevin
downs a hot meal.

He asks if I'd heard
he'd been mugged.
I tell him I had
but that I want to hear

the story from him.
He explains how
the mugger took his Social
Security card, a brand-new

calling card someone
had given him, his last four
dollars. How he can still feel
the guy put a gun to his back

while he's crossing
a downtown parking lot.
How, when Kevin tells him
he's homeless, the guy says,

Give me everything you've got

then runs away
into the dark after taking
the gloves bunched up like fists
in Kevin's jacket pockets.

What the Body Says When There Is No Shelter
After W.S. Merwin's "Some Last Questions"

What do the arms say?
    They took my son away.

What do the legs say?
    Ask the feet.

What do the feet say?
    Distance is measured in eye-lengths.

What do the eyes say?
    Possibility, possibility.

What do the hands say?
    The despair of these tethered birds…

What does the neck say?
    Bend like the grass with dew; sun comes.

What does the head say?
    Don't ask the neck.

What does the belly say?
    Half-empty or half-full?

What do the shoulders say?
    Ask the back.

What does the back say?

What does the back say?

Fringe

verb

6
to serve as a fringe for, or to be arranged around or along so as to suggest a fringe

Use in a sentence:

Though you are invisible, did you know your community decorates the lives of the mainstream?

See marginal

Marginal, adjective

1 c: occupying the borderland of a relatively stable geographic or cultural area

> gray day
> a makeshift tent's blue plastic
> makes a small sky

At Alan's Tent

It's November and Alan says he still hasn't had to use his kerosene heater to warm his tent.

I'm used to the cold. I'm military.

He's originally from Florida but did three years' jail time in Michigan's Upper Peninsula. After he got out, he was taken to a downstate probation facility. He didn't get very far when he was let go with no money, job, or car.

Now, he says, the cooler months will bring in cash from raking leaves and shoveling snow, but he needs to find some warm socks and gloves.

I'm military. You travel on your feet. You got to have dry socks and dry boots.

He says if there were a shelter he'd go there for the winter, but he'd still want to keep his spot here in the woods by the river.

And now I can read your mind. Why would a person want to live like this? I'm a—how do you say it—a recluse, I'm a hermit. It's only temporary. I've been here four years.

But you ought to see this place in the springtime—it's too green! I can't even find myself—it's a tropical paradise. When I sit here on a nice morning and you see the deer, and the birds flying across—it's my house. When things are green. I've seen the mist on the river."

Sunday Dinner

I sit down next to Patty
at one of the soup kitchen's
gingham-covered tables.
There's never any wait:
plates of food appear instantly.
I don't know Patty well,
but she talks nonstop
about her past, cutting
her ham into tiny pieces
and giving me the years
her first husband took from her—
beatings, burns from cigarettes,
darkness in a locked closet.
But it was only their son
who was really taken from her,
she says, when he was put
into foster care. She pauses
to give her knife and fork a rest,
a smile chancing her face.

Soon, she will see
her son for the first time
in 25 years. *I get him
for Mother's Day,* she says.
Father's Day, too.

Fringe

See marginal

Marginal, adjective
1: written or printed in the margin of a page

        the exhausted verbs
            of your feet—
   one grammar to another

a: of, relating to, or situated at a margin or border

            between the freeway
            and the strip mall—
            tent city

b: not of central importance
also: limited in significance or status

       none of the above

2: characterized by the incorporation of habits and values from two
divergent cultures and by incomplete assimilation in either

       Use in a sentence:

           She tries to feed her family from a box
           that won't speak her language

3: excluded from or existing outside the mainstream of society, a group,
or a school of thought

Ex Libris

Bobby. Bobby, the sound of whose
words come out blurred, but true—
a speech impediment that curls
each syllable into a vowelly slur.
Bobby on a sunny late-March morning,
walking right up to the information desk
at the library and saying he wants to learn
how to read, right now, that this is the place,
and something inside falling open. I am there
to help but can't change jobs, can't drop
my duties at the desk, so I look up
the number for a literacy coalition,
a group that works with adults.
While he waits, he recites the *ABC* song,
crooning *W* right after *P*, and smiling
and sighing at the end. I give him
the number and he reluctantly takes it,
disappointed that not one of us clerks
can do what he wants us to:
just sit down with me at a desk
and teach me how to read.
And he leaves, walking past shelf
after shelf of books in colorful jackets
with their backs turned to him.

Lessons

As a girl she'd gone to school until
her breasts began, then was kept home
until married at 17. Five grown kids later
she's here at the literacy center
memorizing transition words—*but why,*
she asks, *does the sentence have to change
course? Can't everything just be simpler?*
Week after week she comes, fifty-some
and struggling to understand the gears and wheels
of the second language her tongue
knows by heart. Together we pull sentences
apart, explore just why it is
this word follows that one. It's all
for a piece of paper, she says,
her GED. She wants a good job—she
who has lived by someone else's book
all her life. *I love to talk,* she says,
and *I'm good with people.*
We talk about supporting points
in an argument and about getting into
a vehicle to get to the meaning
of a metaphor. It takes you places, I say.
She climbs inside, eager to go
wherever learning will take her
out of her husband's house.

Luna/Because

Luna says the problem is darkness,
that it's her disability—
I have to be home by 8.

Because 15 years ago just like yesterday,
the rapist broke into her house while she slept
and started punching my lights out.
And even though she needs you
to hold her at the soup kitchen,
touch is a traitor

and now night is a place
where the razor blade tricks her
into its slick caresses

because men always
seem to want something and they never
mean what they say. Because

she wants to show you her scars:
a galaxy of stars up and down her arms.
Last week she got a new

permanent. *To feel like a woman—*
but she thinks her dark
hair makes her look depressed

and today she has a coupon
to make herself blonde.
She's grateful for the Dollar Tree,

where she can buy something
to feel pretty.
Is that too much to ask? She asks anyway,

because the disability check
only goes so far.
Night keeps coming back.

Fringe

See marginal

Marginal, adjective

*4 b(1): having a character or capacity fitted to yield a supply of goods which when marketed at existing price levels will barely cover the cost of production—*marginal *land*

> autumn leaves follow
> the runaway inside—
> revolving doors

4 b(2): of, relating to, or derived from goods produced and marketed with such result: marginal *profits*

> chilly morning
> a man works the off-ramp
> asking for work

SEE MORE

> real numbers—
> 553,742 homeless in the U.S.
> on any given night

SEE LESS

Unbroken

I'm arranging my purchases on the front seat and notice the car behind me—a beater black Fiat with tinted windows. I sense someone is in there but can't see inside. I turn back to my hands. Looking up a moment later, I see a young woman with a long ponytail next to the Fiat, doing much as I am—standing outside the open front-passenger-side door, fiddling with something. The young woman's heavily tattooed arms appear to be folding clothes, and I can see inside just enough to tell that the vehicle is stuffed with pillows, boxes, and bags. The smell of stale cigarette smoke drifts over. I instantly make up a story that she's living out of her car and quickly guilt myself for doing so. It's just that I've seen it so many times before—beginning back when I was a stringer for a small-town newspaper, writing about local homelessness and only a paycheck away from it myself. People parked in crowded lots as a way of trying to hide, their cars packed to the gills with their belongings.

I get back to organizing my things, then suddenly hear the woman's voice: "*Noooo!*"—and look over to see a colorful mylar birthday balloon just escaping her hands. For an instant I consider jumping for it—too late. From inside the car, the sound of a small child crying. "Be *quiet!*" the woman yells. I can tell she knows I'm looking her way, but she doesn't meet my eyes. I want to say something comforting to the child, to risk the woman telling me to be quiet too. But I don't. The child cries harder, louder. The balloon quickly becomes a small but persistent speck in the sky.

> circle widening
> on the pond
> first drop of rain

Your Dream Sleep

Even with no face to put to your name
I feel like I'm looking at something
I'm not supposed to. Filing the mail
is one of my new jobs here at the shelter,
and in your folder I've just placed
a queen-sized, glossy, padded envelope
on which a pajamaed couple is smiling,
lounging on the famous mattress
in the wake of a refreshing night's sleep
that will send them off to a day's
fulfilling work and bring them

home again to this—being
a confident woman, happy in love,
a radiant man, gentle and affectionate.
They make it look so easy, doing whatever
it takes to afford the evening's
delights, mattress of everything-you-ever-
wanted-in-your-life—and I'm looking

while adrift from a foot-weary day
in which you have not been back
to check your mail, the pale rectangle
bearing your name and this address float
like a tiny rowboat on the champagne-satin
sea of their bliss among the words
the softest most comfortable rest
you'll ever know

Long Lonesome Lonely Road

Ralph has a gift for jigsaw puzzles and loves to tease the volunteers at the soup kitchen. He wears mixed plaids and pennies in his penny loafers.

He says his sisters in Coldwater scold it's the country-western music that gets him down: Ernie Tubbs, Hank Williams, Jr., Jimmy Rogers—part of him from way back when, coming over the radio in Jackson prison. He penciled the lyrics on the cell wall and copied them neatly onto lined paper—he still has them all. Nothing else to do those 25 years, he says, except take "civil defense courses." That was 25 years ago.

Now Ralph lives his life like a country-western song. At 72, with poor health and few job skills, he can't pay his bills. And Sheryl, the younger sister of his common-law wife, Ruth, *is the most beautiful woman in the world*, but Sheryl turns a deaf ear.

She's the reason I rode my bike out in front of a truck on Highway 223, Ralph says, lovestruck.

He's been going through the old lyrics again. He said he heard a new song on the radio and started writing the words on a cardboard box but can't remember how it ends.

I'm on a long road, he scrawls in a letter to Sheryl. *I'm on a crazy, long, lonesome lonely road.*

2: Walls

"The American criminal justice system holds almost 2.3 million people in 1,833 state prisons, 110 federal prisons, 1,772 juvenile correctional facilities, 3,134 local jails, 218 immigration detention facilities, and 80 Indian Country jails as well as in military prisons, civil commitment centers, state psychiatric hospitals, and prisons in the U.S. territories."

—Prison Policy Initiative, March 2020

Fringe

noun

4
something regarded as peripheral, marginal, secondary, or extreme
in relation to something else

Use in a sentence:

(You are) relative to the dominant culture (regarded as)
pushing the (peripheral) edge living the (marginal)
edge becoming the (secondary) edge the (extreme)
cutting edge.

SEE MORE

5
fringe benefit.
(1) benefits, such as free insurance, paid vacation, a 401(k), etc.
received by an employee in addition to regular pay.

N/A

SEE LESS

N/A

Broken, Entering

They divest you
of your immediate past,
emptying you
of your belongings
and leaving you be
with your longings—
this is what you will
measure time with
starting *now*.

*

Even your shadow
must follow orders,
fall in line. But it's the only
thing they can't take,
can't make wear a number.

It hides in broad
daylight, comes out again
when the hours grow long
and thin in the Yard.

*

Candy is currency;
paper, pencils—prized
possessions. The guards
watch for every sign
that you are getting
comfortable again.

*

Each night you escape
into sleep and a recurring
dream about living
under a heavy rock
with black-and-white photos
of people and things
that have already changed.

*

And you wake, both dreading
and looking forward to
the visits, the faces
from home that keep
bringing expressions
you've never seen before.

Prison Triptych

I Captive

They arrest you,
as in a full stop.
They take you in,
and you are surrounded.
They give you a number,
which you will always keep
close to your name.
They put you in a cage
and you are told it is your place.
They turn you into a clock,
ticking off the years
one second at a time.

II Enculturation

In a desert of bars and walls
your tattoos are code;
whispers, a new set of rules;
glances, a whole conversation.
You follow a timetable that is always
one step ahead of you, a schedule
you make your own out of necessity.
In your room is a narrow bunk,
a table bolted to the floor,
and a calendar that is both friend
and foe, issuing each day
a number and placing it in solitary,
then burying it in its own
private box. You mark each
with an X at its passing.

III Hope

After three years you know
what has been taken
out of you for good, and what
never will be. What is left
has become a point of contention
between you and these walls,
the day's duties, and Time,
which guards your every move.
You envy the shape-changing moon,
lobbed over the open sky of the Yard
month after month. With only two-
and-a-half years to go, you can't recall
when you began enjoying
the food. You start looking forward
to chores, going to class.
Still, whatever you are doing,
you always want to leave early.

Fringe

See marginal

Marginal, adjective

4a: close to the lower limit of qualification, acceptability, or function: barely exceeding the minimum requirements

N/A

prison math class—
he signs his homework
with his number

Prison Literature Class

Like the pages of their rented textbooks,
each student carries himself inside
a private, portable container
to protect his skin
from the walls of this place.

*

They bow their heads to the exam
I've given them on *The Importance
of Being Earnest* while spring kildeer cry
beyond the window cracked
to release the captive air.

Although they know I know their names,
each adds his number to every sheet,
double proof of identity:
once from the outside in
twice from the inside out.

*

I give them homework assignments
and take-home quizzes
and they all pass
even though home is never
where they do them.

*

They tell me they've got nothing but time
and they serve it, the movement
of their blood doling out seconds and years
while they learn a new trade:
making pages from hours and walls.

In their weekly journal they all write
about the things they miss—the women
and men, the children they want to have
give them another chance, the dreams
they know they had last night,
which now escape them.

One writes about the walls he walks
inside these walls inside himself
and how something in him
does not love them
and something in him
cannot bear to bring them down.

Another writes a poem about a kiss
between an inmate and his visitor—
a kiss that everyone witnessed,
even the guards. It was a kiss so long
and so real that by the end of it,
the prisoner was a free man.

The Poem Speaks to the Prisoner
—*after Tyehimba Jess*

It always starts with home—
how much time until then
and how much hope along the way.
You've just learned how
to use your fingers for
purposes like me, and at such
a risk, too, with no privacy.
Is Hope a thing with feathers
or a blade? A key? A frame
full of glass but no picture? A sun
that leaves you day after day?
In between the figures
you've discovered a crack
in the cinderblock.

Fringe

See marginal

Marginal, adjective
*5: relating to or being a function of a **random variable** that is obtained from a function of several random variables by integrating or summing over all possible values of the other variables*

SEE MORE

> hold fast to dreams—
> a kitchen glove flutters
> in the razor wire

random variable
The formal mathematical treatment of random variables is a topic in <u>probability theory</u>. In that context, a random variable is understood as a <u>measurable function</u> defined on a <u>probability space</u> that maps from the <u>sample space</u> to the real numbers.—Wikipedia

> real numbers—
> 2.3 million in the United States
> behind bars

SEE LESS

Special Thanks

A very special thank you goes to Laz Slomovits for encouraging me to create this book. In addition, his helpful suggestions, feedback, proofreading, and all-around support truly made it possible. Mucho amor!

Thank you to Lisa Fay Coutley for her detailed feedback on the manuscript and encouragement to get it published.

I also want to thank the members of the Tornado Wine poetry writing group for their feedback on some of the poems in *Fringe*, as well as the Evergreen Haiku Study Group for helping shape my journey as a haiku writer.

Much gratitude goes to Larry Smith, Director, Bottom Dog Press; Kevin Walzer, Poetry Editor, and Lori Jareo, Business Editor, of Cherry Grove Collections; past and present editors of Plain View Press; and editor Christen Kinkade and the other staff at Finishing Line Press.

And many, many thanks go to the following organizations: The Daily Telegram (Adrian, Michigan), The Daily Bread of Lenawee soup kitchen, the Shelter Association of Washtenaw County, Detroit Friendship House, Siena Literacy Center (Detroit, Michigan), the Jackson College Corrections Education Program, and the Ann Arbor District Library—we are all better off for what you do! Thank you for giving me the opportunity to enter into, and better understand, the lives of the people you serve.

Also by Jennifer Burd

Daily Bread: *A Portrait of Homeless Men & Women of Lenawee County, Michigan*

Body and Echo

Day's Late Blue

Receiving the Shore (with Laszlo Slomovits)

Jennifer **Burd** is the author of two full-length books of poetry, *Days Late Blue* and *Body and Echo*, and a previous chapbook/CD, *Receiving the Shore*, of some of her seasonal poetry set to music by Laszlo Slomovits. *Fringe* is her first chapbook with Finishing Line Press. She is also author of a book of creative nonfiction, *Daily Bread: A Portrait of Homeless Men & Women of Lenawee County, Michigan*. She is co-author (with Laszlo Slomovits) of a children's play based on Patricia Polacco's book *I Can Hear the Sun*, which was produced by Wild Swan Theatre of Ann Arbor, Michigan. She received an MFA in creative writing from the University of Washington and has taught literature classes at Jackson Community College in Jackson, Michigan, and creative writing classes through The Loft Literary Center, Minneapolis. Jennifer has also worked as a job developer, editor, newspaper reporter, library clerk, literacy tutor, and instructional designer.

Jennifer's employment experiences inspired many of the pieces in *Fringe*. As a reporter for *The Daily Telegram* in Adrian, Michigan, she contributed to an award-winning series of articles on homelessness after spending months interviewing homeless individuals at a local soup kitchen and on the streets. Part of her work as an English literature instructor for Jackson Community College included teaching prison inmates working toward a college degree. As a writer and photographer for Detroit Friendship House, a food pantry and resource center located in Hamtramck, Michigan, she interviewed clients facing poverty and/or who were newly arrived immigrants seeking resources while working to attain citizenship status. As a volunteer literacy tutor for Siena Literacy Center in Detroit, Jennifer coached community members seeking to improve their English reading and writing skills.

Some of Jennifer's other interests include metaphor studies, reading and writing haiku, and collaborative writing projects. She is also a Certified Forest Therapy Guide. Her website is at jenniferburd.ink.